PIANO ACCOMPANIMENT

Folk Strings

Piano Accompaniment
Arranged and Edited by Joanne Martin

Contents

Swing Low, Sweet Chariot	2
My Grandfather's Clock	4
Moo-Lee-Hua	6
Alouette	8
Marianina	10
Don't You Go	14
Farewell to Nova Scotia	16
Yankee Doodle	18
Valencianita	20
She's Like the Swallow	22

Cover Design: Candy Woolley
Illustrations: Rama Hughes

© 2002 Summy-Birchard Music
division of Summy-Birchard Inc.
Print rights administered by
Alfred Publishing Co., Inc.
All Rights Reserved Printed in U.S.A.
ISBN 1-58951-158-1

Any duplication, adaptation or arrangement of the compositions contained in this collection requires the written consent of the Publisher.
No part of this book may be photocopied or reproduced in any way without permission. Unauthorized uses are an infringement of the U.S. Copyright Act and are punishable by law.

SWING LOW, SWEET CHARIOT

United States
Arranged by JOANNE MARTIN

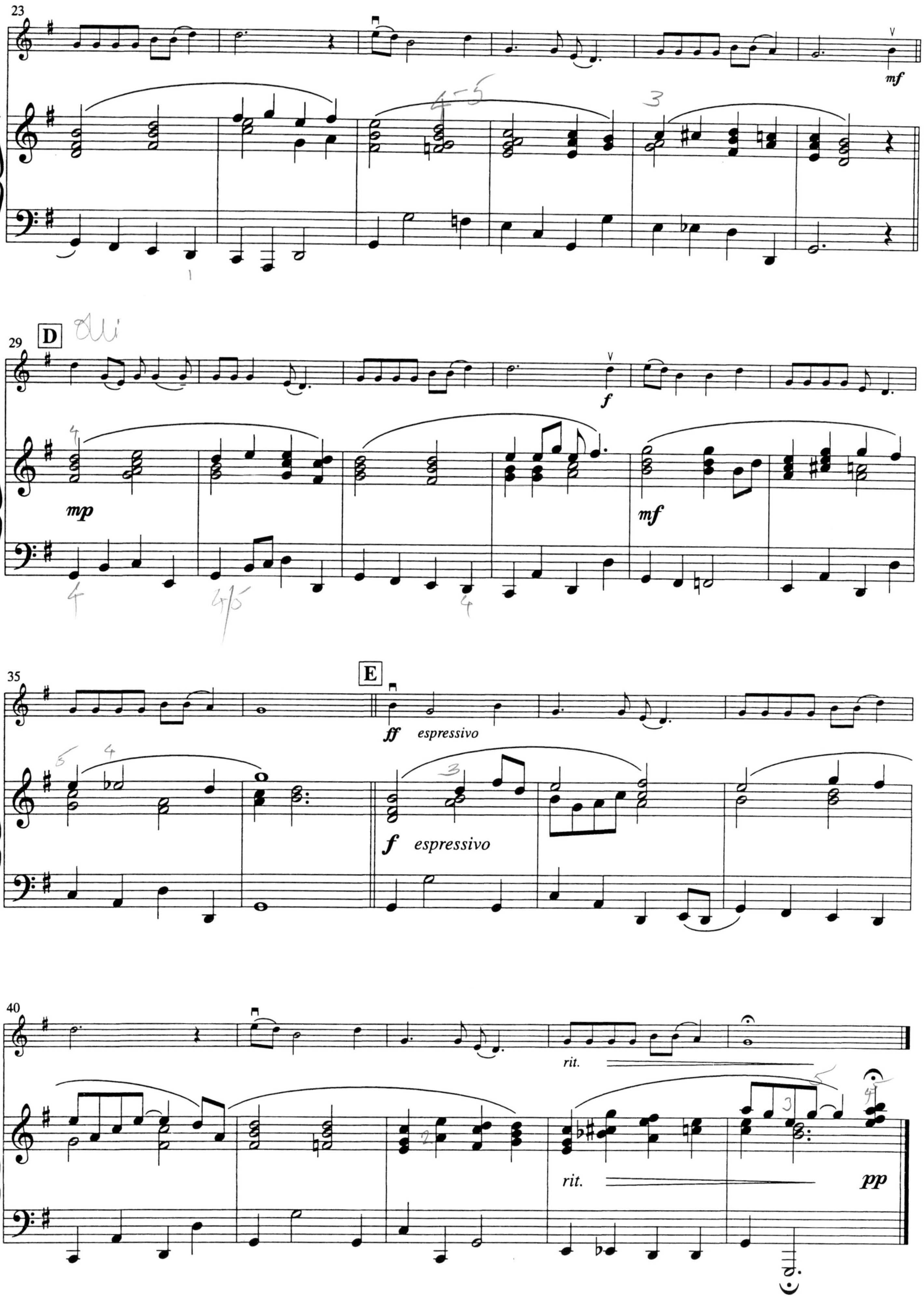
23
mf
29
D
mp
f
mf
35
E
ff espressivo
f espressivo
40
rit.
rit.
pp

MY GRANDFATHER'S CLOCK

Henry Clay Work
Arranged by JOANNE MARTIN

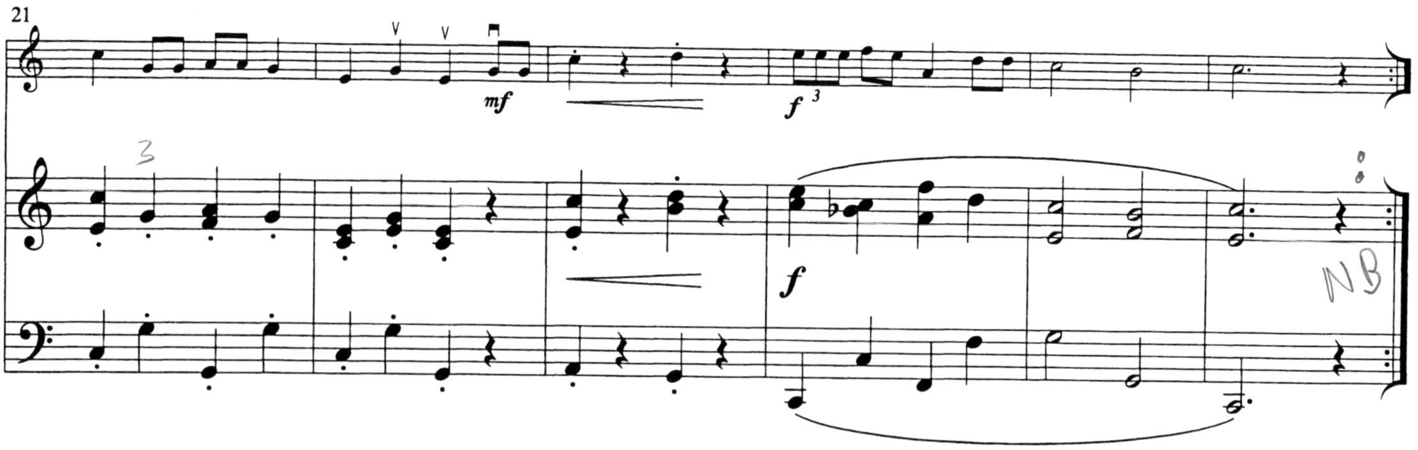
21
mf
f
3
f

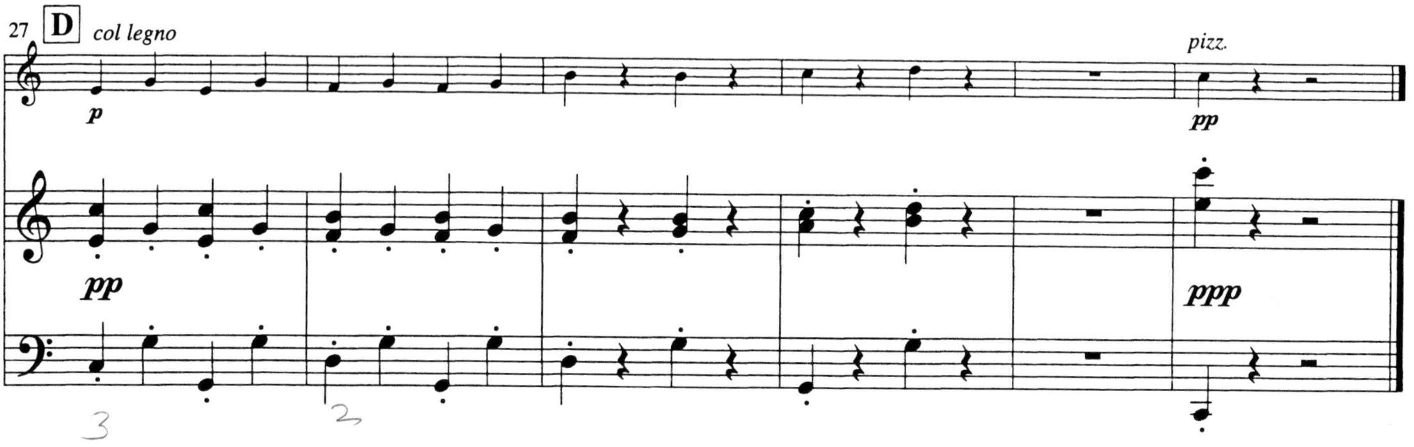
27
D
col legno
p
pizz.
pp
pp
ppp

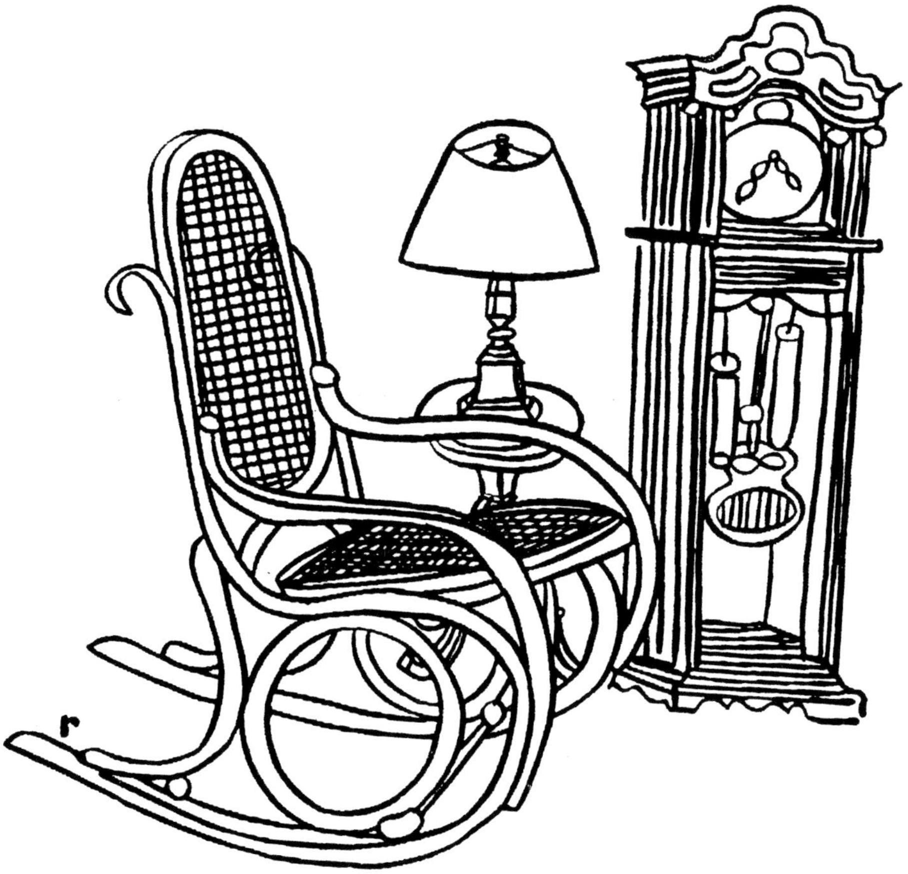

MOO-LEE-HUA

China
Arranged by JOANNE MARTIN

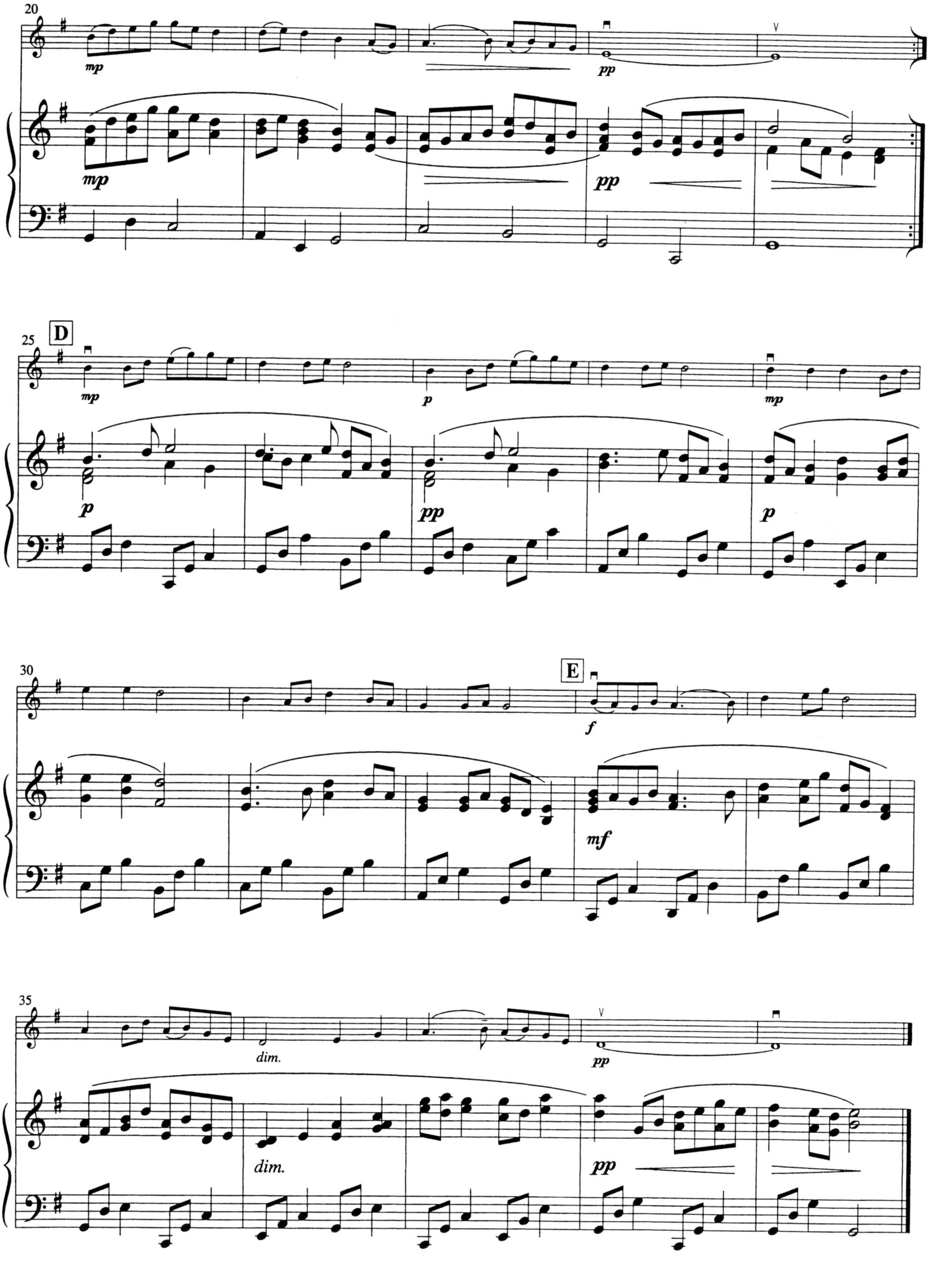
20
mp
pp
25
D
mp
p
30
E
f
mf
35
dim.
pp

ALOUETTE

Canada
Arranged by JOANNE MARTIN

Allegro giocoso ♩ = 80

Alouette - 2

MARIANINA

Italy
Arranged by JOANNE MARTIN

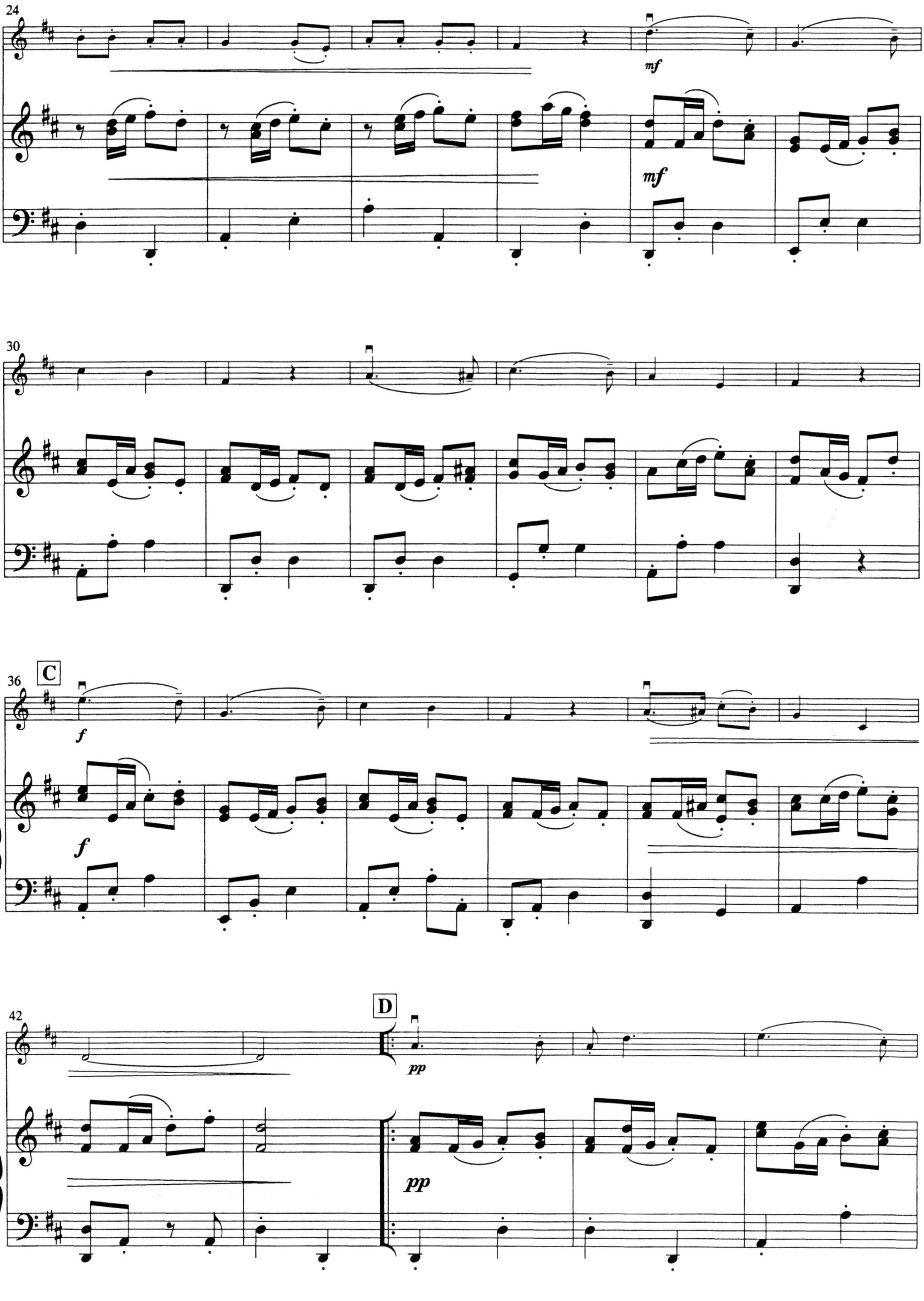
24
mf
mf
30
C
36
f
f
42
D
pp
pp

12

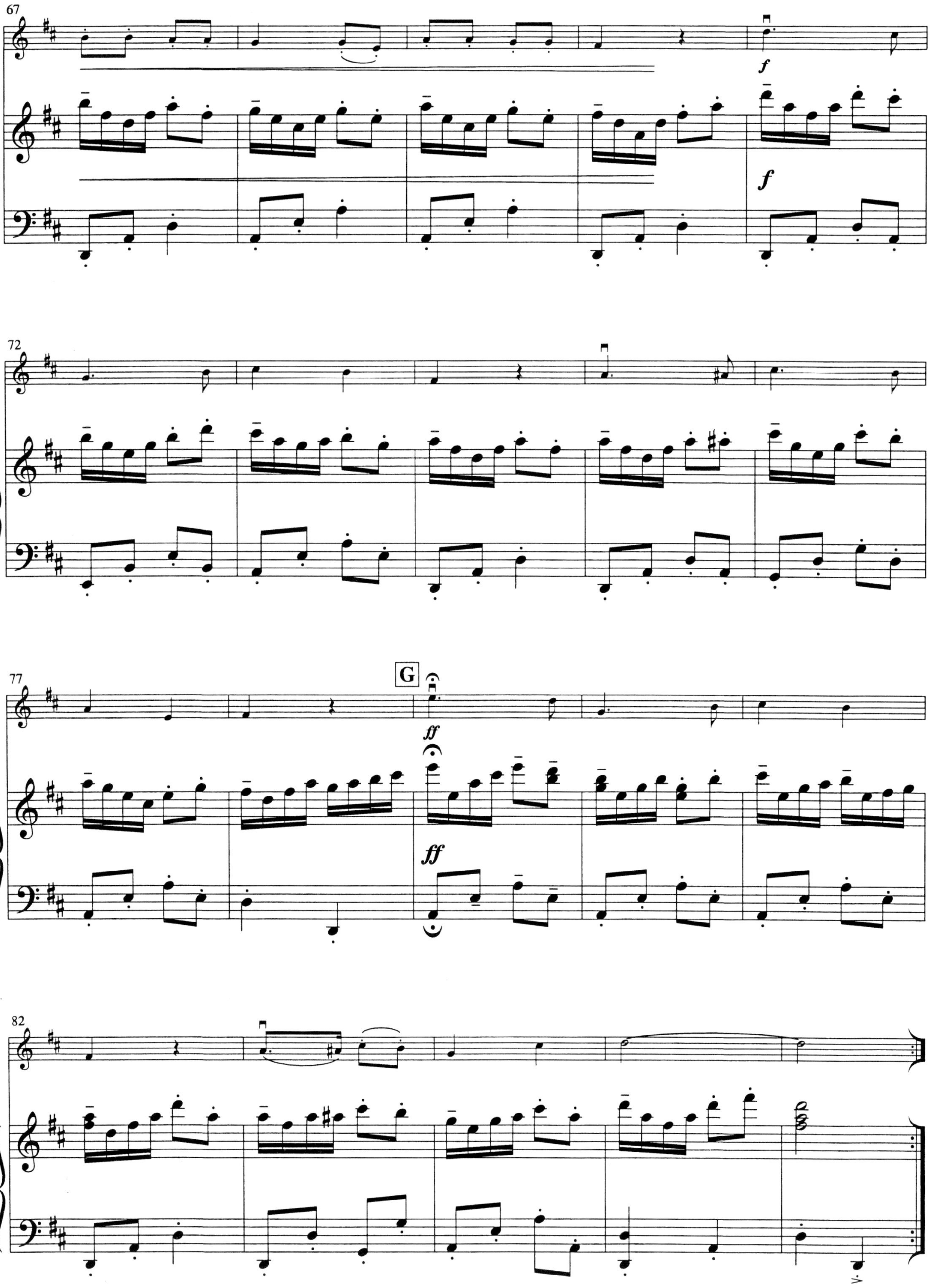
67
f
f
72
77
G
ff
ff
82

DON'T YOU GO

Philippines
Arranged by JOANNE MARTIN

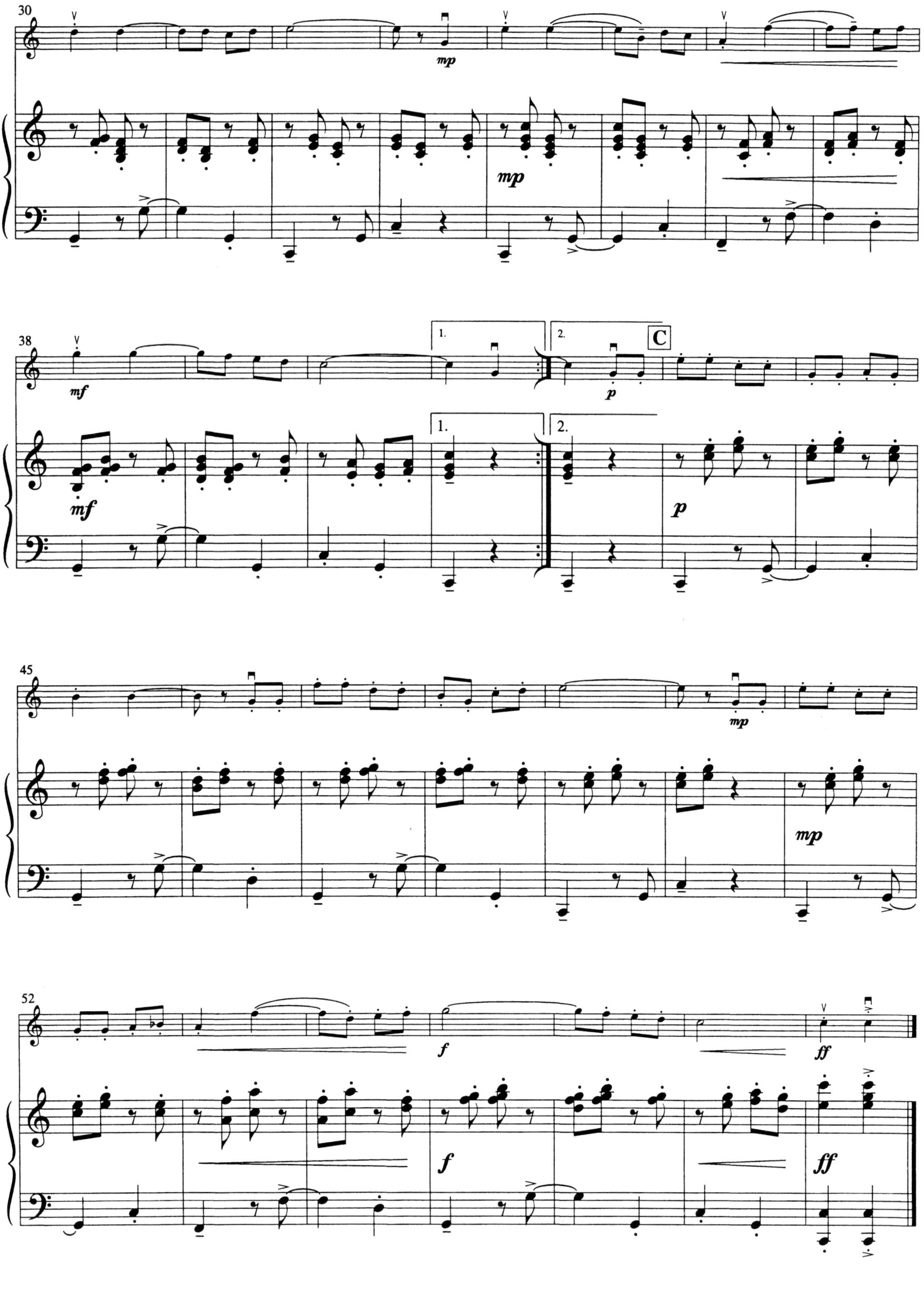
30
mp
38
mf
1.
2.
C
p
45
52
f
ff

FAREWELL TO NOVA SCOTIA

Canada
Arranged by JOANNE MARTIN

Farewell to Nova Scotia - 2

YANKEE DOODLE

United States
Arranged by JOANNE MARTIN

Yankee Doodle - 2

VALENCIANITA

Venezuela
Arranged by JOANNE MARTIN

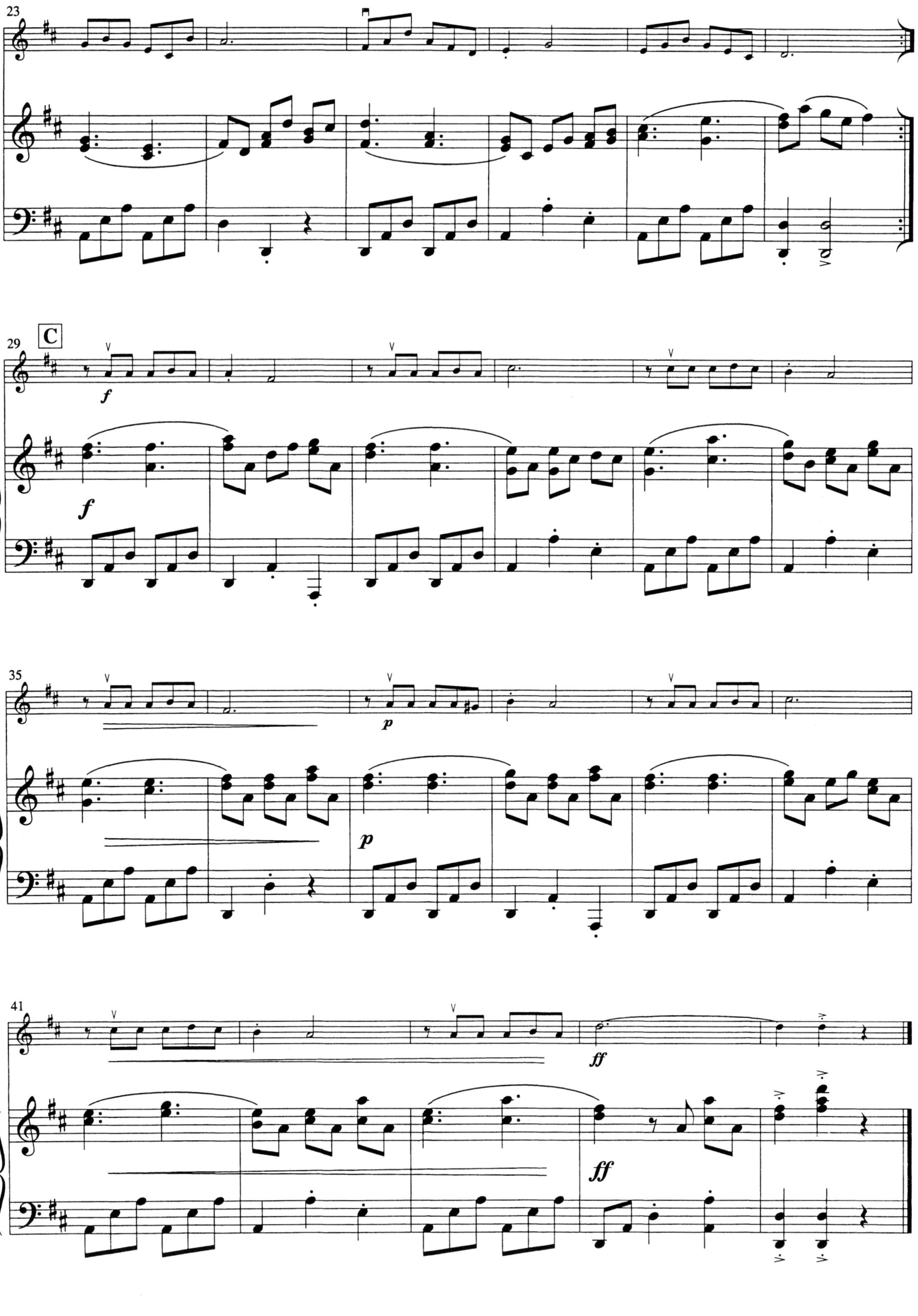
C

SHE'S LIKE THE SWALLOW

Canada
Arranged by JOANNE MARTIN

She's Like the Swallow - 2

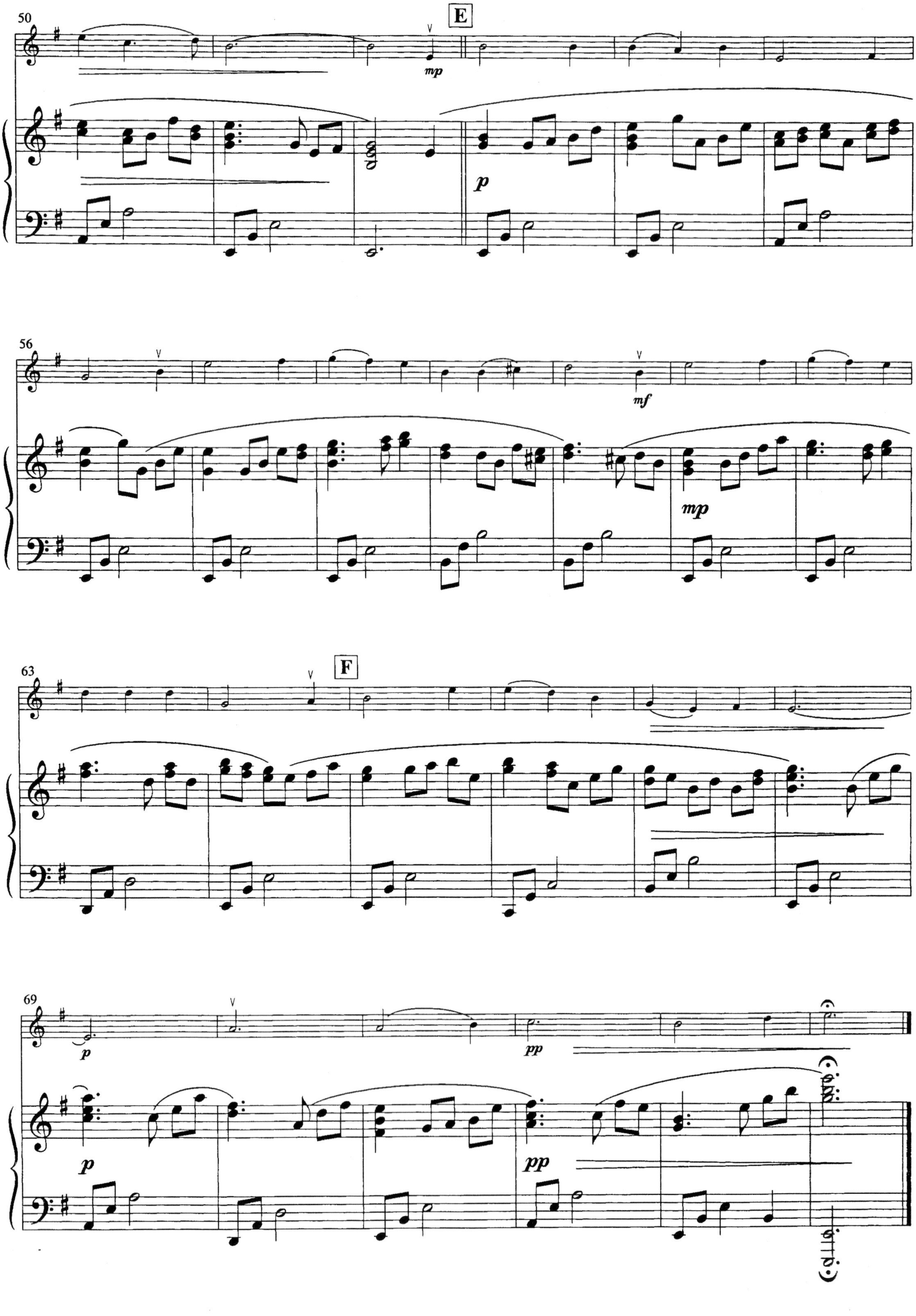
50
E
mp
p
56
mf
mp
63
F
69
p
pp
p
pp